Warning: Wildfires

Calling all aliens!

Are you planning a holiday to planet Earth?

Finn and Zeek are here to help.

'Warning: Wildfires'
Published by MAVERICK ARTS PUBLISHING LTD

Suite 1, Hillreed House, 54 Queen Street,
Horsham, RH13 5AD, +44 (0)1403 256941
© Maverick Arts Publishing Limited August 2024

A CIP catalogue record for this book is available at the British Library.

ISBN 978-1-83511-014-0

Printed in India

www.maverickbooks.co.uk

Credits:
Finn & Zeek illustrations by Jake McDonald, Bright Illustration Agency
Cover: Jake McDonald/Bright, © Arnold John Labrentz/Shutterstock
Inside: © My Photo Buddy/Shutterstock (6), © John Crux/Shutterstock (7), © stockpexel/Shutterstock (7), © Eugene R Thieszen/Shutterstock (7), © Richard Whitcombe/Shutterstock (8), © Toa55/Shutterstock (9), © Bruno Ismael Silva Alves/Shutterstock (9), © Tongra239/Shutterstock (10-11), © Kenneth Keifer/Shutterstock (12), © Ralf Lehmann/Shutterstock (13), © ppa/Shutterstock (15), © SvetlanaSF/Shutterstock (16-17), © Mark Carthy/Shutterstock (18), © SherSS/Shutterstock (19), © javi4x4/Shutterstock (20-21), © Toa55/Shutterstock (22), © Toa55/Shutterstock (23), © Avula Kodanda Raghuveer/Shutterstock (24-25), © Marius Dobilas/Shutterstock (27)

This book is rated as: Purple Band (Guided Reading)

Warning: Wildfires

Contents

Introduction	6
Fuel for Fire	10
Things Needed	10
Natural Causes	12
Human Causes	14
Wildfire Effects	16
Bad	16
Good	18
Controlling Fires	20
When to Burn	20
Firefighters	22
Climate Change	24
Future Fires	24
Quiz	28
Index/Glossary	30

INCOMING MESSAGE

Dear Finn and Zeek,

I want to go to Earth but I have heard there are sometimes big fires there! Please can you teach me about them?

Thank you!

From,
Heet
(Planet Dri)

Introduction

Wildfires are large fires which are out of control. They can get so big that they cover millions of acres!

An acre is an area about half the size of a football pitch. That's pretty big!

Wildfires occur in different places around the world including:

Wildfires have been happening for millions of years, but they can be caused or made worse by human actions.

There are different forms wildfires can take.

Ground Fire

This is when a wildfire burns plants in the ground (such as roots). Ground fires can grow into surface or crown fires.

Surface Fire

This is when a wildfire burns plants and leaves on the surface of the ground.

Crown Fire

This is when a wildfire burns in treetops and shrubs.

Fuel for Fire   Things Needed

This 'fire triangle' shows the three things needed for a wildfire to start: heat, fuel and **oxygen**.

Hot, dry and windy weather helps a wildfire to grow. Hot weather dries out plants, which means they burn easier, making fuel for the fire. Winds supply the fire with more oxygen, making it spread faster.

The size and type of plants can affect how a wildfire burns. Some types of plants have oil in them, which makes them burn quicker.

The shape of the land is also important. Fire spreads more easily uphill than downhill.

Sunflowers and olive trees are examples of plants that have oil in them.

Fuel for Fire | Natural Causes

Now let's see what can cause wildfires to start in the first place.

Natural Causes

Lightning can cause wildfires by setting fire to dry plants.

> Some scientists think **climate change** may lead to a bigger risk of wildfires caused by lightning.

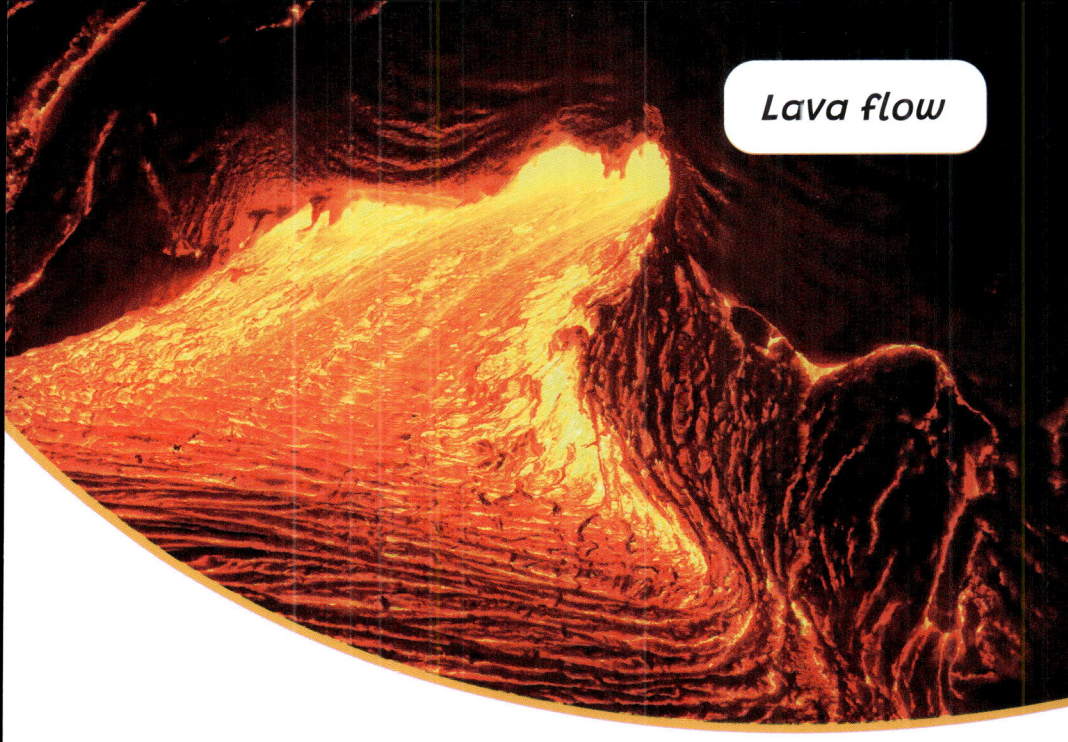

Lava flow

Another possible natural cause is called **spontaneous** heating. This is when dry plants get so hot they catch fire on their own.

Wildfires can even be caused by lava or ash from volcanic eruptions!

Fuel for Fire — Human Causes

Most wildfires nowadays are caused by humans. Many fires are started by accident. Human causes of wildfires include:

- Out of control campfires
- Matches left lying around
- Fireworks
- Sparks from railways
- Arson (a crime where people set fire to things on purpose)

> Always be extra careful if you're making a campfire outdoors. Never leave it without making sure the fire is completely out!

Wildfire Effects — Bad

As we learnt earlier, wildfires have been happening for millions of years. They can have a mix of good and bad effects. Let's start by looking at the bad effects.

Wildfires can be dangerous to humans and animals. They can damage people's houses and property as well as animal habitats.

Haze from a wildfire near San Francisco

Important things like roads, power supplies, water supplies and crops can also be threatened.

The damage caused by wildfires can be very expensive.

Wildfires can even affect climate change by releasing carbon dioxide, a **greenhouse gas!**

Wildfire Effects | Good

Not all the effects of wildfires are bad though. Sometimes they can benefit **ecosystems**!

✓ By clearing some plants, wildfires make space for sunlight to reach others, helping them to grow.

✓ Burnt plants can be good for the soil.

✓ Wildfires can kill diseases and insects that damage trees.

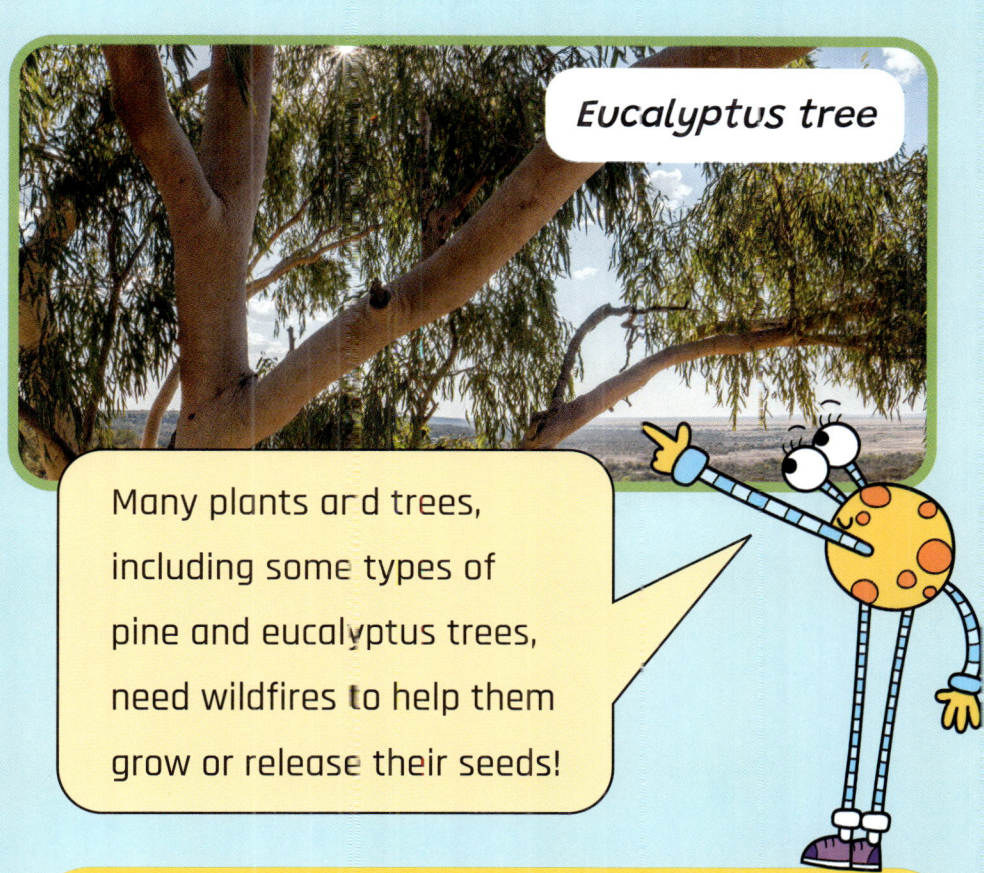

Eucalyptus tree

Many plants and trees, including some types of pine and eucalyptus trees, need wildfires to help them grow or release their seeds!

Animals can benefit from wildfires:

- Some birds can hunt prey trying to escape the fires on the ground.
- When new plants grow after wildfires, they provide habitats and food for many different animals.

Controlling Fires — When to Burn

Sometimes, fires are started on purpose. These are called prescribed fires. They are used to benefit an ecosystem or to remove fuel for future wildfires. They are heavily controlled!

Fire break

When wildfires are a danger to people, there are many ways they can be **suppressed**.

Remember the 'fire triangle' from earlier? Removing the heat, fuel or oxygen feeding a wildfire is key to bringing it under control.

Plants can be removed from certain areas to form fire breaks (a strip of land without plants). Without plants for fuel, it is harder for a wildfire to spread from one place to another. Things such as wide rivers and roads can act as fire breaks!

Controlling Fires   Firefighters

Firefighters fight wildfires with water to reduce the heat of the fire. Planes and helicopters are sometimes used to drop water and special chemicals called fire retardants on the flames.

Fire retardants are mainly a mixture of water and fertilizer. They make it harder for things to catch fire.

Some wildfires are very difficult for firefighters to bring under control. People may need to leave their homes if a wildfire is a danger to them!

Climate Change Future Fires

Climate change is having a big effect on wildfires. It is making them more likely to happen and more likely to be serious.

Hotter and drier weather because of climate change means a bigger risk of wildfires. Remember: heat dries out plants, making them ideal fuel!

Wildfires also affect climate change! They add to **global warming** by releasing carbon dioxide (a greenhouse gas) when they burn.

When wildfires destroy forests, they also reduce the amount of carbon dioxide that can be absorbed by trees. This means there is more carbon dioxide in the air, adding to global warming!

MESSAGE SENT

Dear Heet,

Wildfires do happen on Earth but humans have many ways of trying to manage them.

If you decide to make a campfire, remember to be careful and make sure it is completely out before leaving it!

From,
Finn and Zeek :)

This helicopter is dropping water on a wildfire in Norway!

Quiz

1. Which of these is not a form of wildfire?

a) Crown fire

b) Top fire

c) Ground fire

2. Which of these is not in the 'fire triangle'?

a) Oxygen

b) Water

c) Heat

3. Which of these is a natural cause of wildfires?

a) Lightning

b) Arson

c) Fireworks

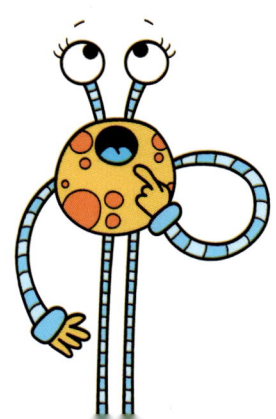

4. What is a fire break?

a) A chemical used to put fires out

b) A tool used to clear vegetation

c) A strip of land without plants

5. What are fire retardants?

a) Things which catch fire easily

b) Chemicals which help to put out fires

c) Strips of land without plants

6. Which greenhouse gas is released during wildfires?

a) Carbon dioxide

b) Oxygen

c) Water

Turn over for answers

Index/Glossary

Climate Change pg 12, 17, 24, 25
Long-term changes to the Earth's weather and climate.

Ecosystem pg 18, 20
A natural environment and everything that lives in it.

Global Warming pg 25
The warming of the Earth's climate due to a build-up of greenhouse gases in the atmosphere.

Greenhouse Gas pg 17, 25
A gas which traps heat in the Earth's atmosphere.

Oxygen pg 10, 21
A gas which many living things need to breathe.

Quiz Answers:

1. b, 2. b, 3. a, 4. c, 5. b, 6. c

Spontaneous pg 13

Something that happens on its own, without anything else causing it.

Suppressed pg 21

When something is fought and weakened.

Book Bands for Guided Reading

The Institute of Education book banding system is a scale of colours that reflects the various levels of reading difficulty. The bands are assigned by taking into account the content, the language style, the layout and phonics. Word, phrase and sentence level work is also taken into consideration.

Maverick Early Readers are a bright, attractive range of books covering the pink to white bands. All of these books have been book banded for guided reading to the industry standard and edited by a leading educational consultant.

Fiction

Non-fiction

To view the whole Maverick Readers scheme, visit our website at www.maverickearlyreaders.com

Or scan the QR code above to view our scheme instantly!